28135

God and Word

GOD *and* WORD

by GERHARD EBELING

FORTRESS PRESS · PHILADELPHIA

Translated by James W. Leitch from the German
Gott und Wort by Gerhard Ebeling
J. C. B. Mohr (Paul Siebeck), Tübingen, 1966

Library of Congress Catalog Card Number 67-14623

3967A67   Printed in U.S.A.   1-91

FOREWORD

These chapters were first prepared as the Earl Lectures given at the Interdenominational Pastoral Conference conducted by the Pacific School of Religion at Berkeley, California, February 15-17, 1966.

My gratitude for the generosity expressed in the invitation of the Pacific School of Religion, the oldest theological institution west of the Mississippi River, an institution which celebrated its centennial in 1966, is matched only by my appreciation for the atmosphere of openness and flexibility which, despite the difficult problems of this nation, makes every visit to the United States an enriching and happy experience. I am especially happy for the opportunity to renew old friendships and to make new ones at many stops along the way.

I regret, however, that I was not able to renew my friendship with Carl Michalson, who had been professor of systematic theology at Drew University in Madison, New Jersey. On November 8, 1965 he was taken from his indefatigable life for others in a plane crash near Cincinnati, Ohio. In preparing these Earl Lectures I found myself engaged in inner conversation with him. Somewhat later I received new insight from an ordination sermon which he had preached two weeks before his death. The sermon dealt with the power of the Word of God. When in that sermon he comes to the word, "God," he says: "That's what the word does—it doesn't point to a thing but creates a situation." It is to the memory of this theologian that these lectures are dedicated.

Zurich, Switzerland   GERHARD EBELING
August 2, 1966

TABLE OF CONTENTS

I.

THE WORD OF
THE GODLESS

The subject "God and Word" is of my own choosing, but I must confess that it involves me in a presumptuous, hazardous, and yet also a necessary project.

The presumptuousness of the project becomes clear to us the moment we recognize that the brief monosyllables "God" and "word" point us into the realm of the boundless. When we deal with God, we deal with the immeasurable, whether it is then said that "God lives" or that "God is dead." And when we enter into the question of the nature of "word," the question of language as the point at which all dimensions of our experience of reality intersect, then we find ourselves in the realm of the inexhaustible, whether that be interpreted as a sign of our power or of our impotence. How are we ever to do justice to these two overwhelmingly complex problems? And how are we to consider them together?

The project is, furthermore, hazardous. Between the two principle terms there stands the word "and," simultaneously joining and separating those terms. The impression is of a harmless juxtaposition of two factors, as if each of the two, God and word, was already established in itself and there remained only our inquiry into their relationship. It seems self-evident to us that it is the language which we command as human beings that gives us the standard by which we even talk of God, and also, on the contrary, that God, insofar as he really exists, is independent of our talk of him. But what if the facts are otherwise, and there prevails between God and word a tension which the particle "and" is inadequate to bear? What if the "and" which links them breaks down, so that God is left without word and our word without God, a wordless God and godless word—and thus the place of God is taken by a silence that renders us speechless, smothering every sound and even every thought, while our word ultimately fails and falls silent? Or what if an all too close contact between God and word results in a melting of the "and" which separates them, so that we read, "the Word was God" (John 1:1), and consequently what is to be expected of the word is no less than God? This, too, could be extremely hazardous—provided that familiarity with the language of the Bible does not keep us from thinking about it. Let us only try to realize what it means that God actually comes to grips with us through a word, and to understand that we are expected to represent God to the world by means of our word! It is understandable that even a man like Isaiah was appalled: "Woe is me! For I am lost; for I am a man of unclean lips, and I dwell in the midst of a people of unclean lips" (Isaiah 6:5).

And yet I do believe that despite all our misgivings the subject "God and Word" is necessary, in fact vitally necessary. For, although this may be surprising, we threaten to die of language poisoning. This is not because God has completely vanished from our language, but because God is festering in our language.

Our language—it is vastly more than familiar vocabulary or rules of usage. Language is the body of our spirit. The life of language goes on as we receive tradition and convert it again into words for which we ourselves can answer. Two factors—on the one hand, all that we have been taught by parents, by those about us, and by earlier generations, all that has thus entered into us or lies ready for us in a vast warehouse of printed matter; and on the other hand, all that we then can say from personal knowledge and experience, whether publicly, privately, or in the secret places of the heart—these two factors are the poles between which the life of language takes place, grows or wastes away.

Our linguistic tradition is full of references to God. But what *we* are able to say in this respect is little or nothing. It is not merely a question here of the vocable "God," but rather of the entirety of what is to be said of all things in the light of God and before God: how the world and history, my fellows and my own self, my whence and whither, life and death are given expression before God. The Bible was the linguistic home of our forefathers—albeit in various degrees of intensity and understood in conflicting ways—and consequently God was more or less their linguistic center, though not by any means to the exclusion of hypocrisy and blasphemy. That this is the tradition from which we come, no one can deny. But now, in our day, it looks as if talk of God, and all that goes with it, is nothing more than just a tradition, a mere form of speech, a dead relic of the language of the past.

If we do not see this shift in the situation, then there will in fact be a danger of what I have called language poisoning—a sepsis in our spiritual life. This is why the subject "God and Word" is vital, essential to the continuance of life. We must not irresponsibly continue to talk of God, nor irresponsibly stop doing so. Yet to a disquieting extent both things are happening today. And both are poisonous, albeit in different ways.

Talk of God that lacks authenticity, that has become empty and powerless, spells disintegration to faith and thought. On this, whether pious or not, all are fundamentally agreed. And hopefully the non-believers will not be the sole advocates of thought. Whoever takes the holiness of God seriously should make certain that no one is more conscientious than he in the use of words. That

3

has always been so, but it has also always been questioned. Talk of God is word at its most demanding, because it demands pure faith. For this reason such talk is always in danger of becoming presumptuous and incredible.

Now, however, we find ourselves in an age in which responsible talk of God has to satisfy extreme demands. Never before was there so great a gulf between the linguistic tradition of the Bible and the language that is actually spoken. Hence, never before was it so easy to suspect that God is merely a matter of tradition. Never before was the task of answering for God in our word put before us so radically. The problem today, seen as a whole, is indeed not that there is any lack of institutions and publications which provide possibilities for speaking of God. On the contrary, the problem is how a genuine word of God is to be asserted in the midst of this tremendous inflation of existing possibilities.

For that reason, is reflection on the relationship between God and word necessary only for those who have an interest in talking of God or who still expect something from this talk? Is this reflection necessary in order to sharpen the responsibility of those men for such talk, or is it necessary in order to support them, since the burden of such responsibility is too great for them? Even when the circle of those who are immediately concerned is described in such narrow terms, the scope of our subject yet extends far beyond to the widest circles of the public. Whoever ascribes no significance to talk of God will in any event have to take seriously the effects of stale and decaying talk of God upon the surrounding world. Even from the standpoint of radical secularism it would be shortsighted to expect anything from the inner self-disintegration of belief in God, for it is also in secularism's own interest to be confronted with genuine talk of God and not merely with stale, putrefied language. The struggle concerning God and word must be fought out with all possible clarity. Far more than is normally realized, our customary talk of God—dull sermons and pious words which have no bearing on reality and cause us no further thought—has become empty, producing a slow disintegration. The consequences of this are not by any means to be found only in the religious realm, but also are considerable outside of it—namely, in the devaluation of words in general, the debilitation of the responsible use of language. Hence the subject "God and Word" has an urgency for all who consider themselves responsible for our age.

But we must go still a step further. It would poison our language—so I have said—not only if we irresponsibly continued to speak of God, but also if we irresponsibly stopped doing so. The superficial and flippant way in which talk of God is today widely regarded—explicitly or implicitly—as a thing of the past, stands in inglorious contrast to the depth and richness of that tradition from which our age has severed itself but from whose heritage it nevertheless is still nourished. To recognize such a difference of level is of course not to remove the obstacles which today stand in the way of speaking of God. But to reconcile ourselves to that difference as our destiny, without reaching a settlement with the great linguistic tradition in which "God" was the word of all words, means cultural collapse, the danger of spiritual barbarism. If it is really to be our lot that we must live with a language without God, then we ought at least to do so as decent and cultural men, i.e., not in forgetfulness, but with a respect for our own linguistic tradition. Otherwise we carry along with us an unexamined heritage which, even though we do not speak of God any more, nevertheless has about it the decaying stench of what is dead but not buried.

I now go still further and declare that not only does the

linguistic tradition from which we have come oblige even those who consider themselves free of all responsibility for speaking of God to reflect nevertheless on the relation of God and word. I declare also that the thought of our own linguistic responsibility obliges us to reflect on the relationship in question. How do I do justice to the fact that I am enabled to use words and called upon to use words? What is my duty where words are concerned?

If it is really true that thinking about word as such drives us to think about the relation of God and word, then the usual understanding of our subject is turned the opposite way round. Our immediate reaction to the relation of God and word is of course the idea that it is precisely the examination of the linguistic aspect of faith in God that causes embarrassment. Our talk of God allegedly cannot stand being taken strictly at its word. A critical use of words appears to be dangerous for God. I counter this customary view by making the following assertion, which points the direction for the rest of our reflections: it is precisely the consideration of the nature of word that leads to an understanding of what "God" means.

Yet we would not simply set aside the view that comes readiest to mind. It, too, contains some truth, and thus it cannot be disregarded with impunity. I confine myself to one or two aspects which make it clear why a sober evaluation of word appears to have critical, if not disastrous, consequences for the relation to God.

Faith itself knows that it becomes vain when we stop at pious words, at mere talk of God, and do not go on to corresponding deeds which give realization to the word in life. It is not saying "Lord, Lord" that counts, but doing the will of God. This is one of the strongest impulses for that piety which is given classic expression by, for example, Thomas à Kempis in *The Imitation of Christ,* one of the most widely known works in world literature: "Whosoever would fully and feelingly understand the words of Christ, must endeavor to conform his whole life to Christ. What will it avail you to dispute sublimely the Trinity, if you be void of humility and are thereby displeasing to the Trinity? Sublime words surely make a man neither holy, nor just; but a virtuous life makes him dear to God. I had rather feel compunction, than understand the definition thereof. If you did know by heart the whole Bible and the sayings of all the philosophers—what would all that profit you, without the love of God and without grace?" [1]

Understandably enough, unbelief too, and it in particular, has a keen eye for this. It even supposes that piety is essentially nothing but hypocrisy, an idealogical froth that contradicts and destroys real life. It is no accident that the slogan of "practical Christianity" easily changes into the emancipation of practice from Christian doctrine. And out of mistrust of religious words there grows contempt for words as such.

Of course contempt for words stands in sharpest contradiction to Christian faith, especially as understood by the Reformers. This faith lives, as it confesses, from the word of God, and indeed from the word of God as uttered with final validity, from the word become flesh. To be sure, even theology cannot shut its eyes to the fact that here the term "word" is used in a way that breaks the bounds of normal linguistic usage. It even seems to be in the proper interest of theology to turn one's back on the literal understanding of word as an utterance of human speech, in order that God should not be made finite and God's word not confused with the letter. The problem threatens, however, to become the still more acute question of whether the concept of the word of God is not,

[1] *The Imitation of Christ,* chap. I.

strictly speaking, altogether self-contradictory since the fact of the matter is that "word" exists for us only as human word. Do we not in all honesty have to choose between meaning "word" but then not claiming God for it, or meaning "God" but then not ascribing a word to him?

This brings us into the wide field of the problems of religious language as such. Under the influence of general philosophic views of language, these problems are being intensively discussed today, in Europe mainly from the point of the hermeneutic approach, in the Anglo-Saxon realm primarily from the standpoint of linguistic analysis. In the one case the terms are those of the mental or historical sciences; in the other case the terms are those of natural science and logic. The typical leading concepts are "understanding" on the one side and "verification" on the other. How these two strands of contemporary philosophy of language are interrelated, how far they contradict, overlap, or supplement each other, cannot be discussed here.[2] Today, in any event, our subject "God and Word" is normally conceived in terms of those linguistic problems which are characteristic of the man of our time, for he is the victim of linguistic estrangement from his tradition and linguistic confusion among his contemporaries.

The problem is then: How can we understand and verify statements describing that which, as it seems, lies

[2] For an orientation to these issues, see the following: E. Fuchs, *Hermeneutik* (2nd ed.; Bad Cannstatt: Müllerschön, 1958); M. Heidegger, *Unterwegs zur Sprache* (Pfullingen: Neske, 1959); H.-G. Gadamer, *Wahrheit und Methode: Grundzüge einer philosophischen Hermeneutik* (Tübingen: Mohr, 1960); J. O. Urmson, *Philosophical Analysis: Its Development Between the Two World Wars* (Oxford: Oxford University Press, 1956); F. Ferré, *Language, Logic and God* (New York: Harper and Row, 1961); and, K. O. Apel, "Wittgenstein und das Problem des hermeneutischen Verstehens," *Zeitschrift für Theologie und Kirche*, 63 (1966), pp. 49-87.

outside the realm of experience? Insofar as such statements are not discarded altogether as meaningless, they require laborious reflection if they are to be translated into terms of the present understanding of reality. This threatens to rob them of their original immediacy and force. For in relation to God, talk seems today to be condemned from the start to impropriety. Only silence would seem to be appropriate for God. At this point the atheistic secularism of the modern age, for all its profound difference, is strangely close to mysticism. This experience of the incompatibility of God and word must be kept in mind when it comes to assuming responsibility for speaking of God today.

What is the source of this experience? Why are we finding it so difficult, if not indeed impossible, to speak of God today? What has happened to make us and our age different from the men of earlier times?

Our reflections very soon lead us to the observation that our subject has to do with history, or, to be more precise, with our historical situation in which the relation to tradition has become so problematic. Thus "God and Word" is not by any means a timeless subject, as one might suppose. To be sure, we might well say: what is there about the relationship of God and word that should change and make this question so immediately dependent on the situation? God is surely always God, and word always word! Experience, however, contradicts abstract reflections of this kind. And this is eminently significant for our thinking about God and word. Here time, experience, and history also come into play.[3] They lurk, as it were, in the harmless little word "and." For if we would learn more precisely how God is expressed in language,

[3] Cf. my essay, "Zeit und Wort" in E. Dinkler (ed.), *Dankesgabe an R. Bultmann zum 80. Geburtstag* (Tübingen: Mohr, 1964), pp. 341-356.

and thus how God and word unite in such a way that we are dealing not with an empty word but with a word that causes God to be with us and us with God, then we are brought to the important insight that the time is not always right for a word of this kind. And this word is not available at will. Nor by any means does everyone have the right and the power to speak such a word. The "and" between God and word thus marks the place of man in our subject. For it is surely in man that the time and the capacity for such a word must come about. Where else should talk of God take place, and where else should the right to such talk be determined, save in the man who ventures to assume responsibility for such talk?

But our question was not in the first place so general. We did not ask under what conditions it is time to speak of God, or even under what conditions it is at all right to have the vocable "God" on our lips—if our speaking of God is to be at all appropriate to God. Rather, our question was occasioned by a particular experience of history: the experience that although our linguistic tradition was abundantly able to speak of God, our own age has largely lost the courage—many even believe it has altogether forfeited the possibility—to speak of God. What is the significance of this change in the situation?

Some lament the increasing apostasy of the modern age from God. They blame both individuals and social conditions and see the culpable cause in the age's struggle for autonomy, in its limitation to the things of this world, and in its materialistic outlook. Others celebrate as a sign of progress the fact that man has grown up and freed himself from the darkness of religious superstition and has adopted with fascinating success the path of a purely rational, strictly scientific approach to reality. Both views are superficial.

The optimistic interpretation of our emancipation from

God as "enlightenment" suppresses problems which now exist not only as they always did but more intensely than ever. A sober contemplation of the modern age combines an amazement at the triumphs of reason with a horror at the abysmal depths of unreason. In our day we have experienced the frightful reality of unreason, and we must continue to reckon with this possibility as an abiding menace.

The denunciatory interpretation, on the other hand, narrows the matter down to one of morals—as if it all depended on the good will of the individual and as if the greater part of mankind had deteriorated, or even as if the transition to the modern age had been accompanied by something like a second Fall, that both makes the first Fall look like nothing and causes earlier ages to appear in a glorified light. In actual fact, however, we have here a destiny which cannot be altered—much less reversed—at will. We must avoid over-simplified judgments.

On the one hand it has to be emphasized that estrangement from God as a fact in the atheism of modern times—and as interpreted by Friedrich Nietzsche as the death of God, or, to be more precise, as the murder of God by men—is by no means a process which has introduced godlessness into the world for the first time.[4] The phenomenon of godlessness is as old as the phenomenon of religion—not only in the form of manifest violation of the religious law, but also in pious disguise as the veiled and unrecognized hypocrisy of religious self-justification before God. Speech about God does not rule out godlessness; it can itself be abysmally godless. And contrariwise, silence about God is not in itself a sure mark of godlessness.

[4] Cf. my essay, "Die Botschaft von Gott an das Zeitalter des Atheismus," *Monatschrift für Pastoraltheologie,* 52 (1963), pp. 8-24.

On the other hand we must recognize that the phenomenon of godlessness has become extraordinarily aggravated in modern times, because in contrast to earlier ages it now appears more in the open. Godlessness presents itself unveiled, confesses itself in atheistic terms, and considers itself justified as an allegedly radical honesty. At the same time, however, the situation has also become more complicated. The modern age has produced in the course of the process of secularization a completely legitimate and methodologically restricted atheism. This consists in excluding in principle all talk of God wherever we deal with the things that can be calculated, planned, manufactured and controlled by man. Why it was that on the threshold of the modern age man began to explore methodically and consistently all dimensions of the realm of what can be calculated, planned, manufactured and controlled, and to make himself the master of that realm, is a question to which various partial historical answers could be given, which do not solve the riddle or explain the mysterious depths of this historic turning point as such.

This vast process of secularization could ultimately assume the form of atheism only because talk of God had already been deeply blended into the world experience and world order of the former age. In contrast to the modern, secularized age we can call the former age the Christianized age. It was the age in which Christian talk of God was regarded as the precept which dominated all else. Because it was understood as the law of a particular age, Christian talk of God was barely distinguishable from the form of that particular age of the world. Consequently the things of God and the things of man became confusingly tangled. When man awoke to a methodical examination of reality and a systematic exploitation of his own capabilities, his opponent only seemed to be Christian talk of God; in actual fact his opponent was a whole world condition which was imbued with Christian colors. This gave rise to tragic misjudgments. In the name of faith but actually for the protection of an age that was in the process of passing away, false prohibitions were set up. And in the name of unbelief boundaries were overstepped that had been laid down by men of little faith, men who in so doing actually first brought about the understanding and embracing of such defiance as an act of unbelief. This unbelief, to be sure, had no clear understanding of itself.

These references impress on us the duty of avoiding over-simplified judgments when we deal with the question of talk of God. "The Word of the Godless"—this heading which has pointed the way for the first part of our reflections on "God and Word" has accordingly not given us occasion to expose the whole threatening arsenal of so-called atheist propaganda in order that we may now construct against that propaganda a defense which is a match for the attacker. An attitude of this kind would not do justice to our task at all. "The Word of the Godless" leads us, on the contrary, to consider where the real difficulties in the relationship of God and word actually lie.

Can our word be anything other than the word of the godless, if indeed it is the word of men who, precisely according to the verdict of faith, are without exception sinners before God, and who are thus godless in the strict sense of the term? How can a godless man speak of God? What is the experience that drives him to do so and gives him authority to do so? Why must the godless speak of God? It must, it would seem, be a contradictory experience—on the one hand having to speak of God and on the other hand being unable to speak of God. To be sure, this contradictory experience is usually veiled: the godless man does indeed speak of God without sensing

13

the contradiction, be it that as a religious man he makes himself gods after his own image, or be it that he says in his heart, or even with his lips: "There is no God" (Psalm 14:1). The truth of this contr..dictory experience of having to speak of God while not being able to speak of God, appears to be manifest only where it is given to the godless man to recognize himself as godless even though he is at the same time authorized by God to speak of God. True talk of God, then, would be that in which the godless man receives from God the word which contradicts him, the godless—contradicts him so completely that, godless as he is, it imparts God to him.

These possibly enigmatic-sounding formulations describe provisionally the mystery to which the subject "God and Word" would lead us. They stand on a deeper level than that on which we secularized men usually localize the problem. To us the real problem seems to be how traditional talk of God is to justify itself before the bar of our allegedly unequivocal experience of reality. This experience concentrates itself on the impression of the inhumanity, or non-humanity, of God. That may be seen in two respects. For one thing, the modern age's understanding of reality, which takes its bearings on experience, radically eliminates all anthropomorphism from the idea of God. It thereby makes for a dehumanizing of God which does away with the very idea of God. In the second place, the incomprehensible catastrophes in the history of modern times seem to be irreconcilable with the idea of God as the Father who loves men as his children. The old question of theodicy has become so acute that God has turned into a dark, distorted "X" and in such a form can no longer be addressed as God at all. The death of God would then be due to the fact that God is non-human and appears only in inhumanity—precisely thus does he disappear as God,[5] for only on the ground of his humanity can he be addressed as God.

Speaking of God would in actual fact be meaningful and necessary today if this paradoxical experience of God by secularized man, the experience of the God who has disappeared, only obscures, but does not do away with, the other experience of which we have spoken—namely, the contradiction in man himself of having to speak of God and yet being unable to do so.

Thus the question is: Is the word of man today still the word of the godless? Or have man and his language become so radically secularized that they have ceased even to be godless any more? But is it not the case that the man who in this way has ceased to be godless would have ceased to be human? Would the language which no longer stretches to the phenomenon of godlessness, which no longer shows the deep hurt of the contradiction of having to speak of God and yet not being able to—would it not be a dehumanized language? For then the experience of the inhumanity of God would correspond to the inhumanity of man himself, which consists in the fact that man is resigned to the idea that God is inhuman.

So long, however, as our word is still a word of the godless, it is, precisely in virtue of this self-contradiction, witness to God.

[5] This formulation has been suggested in J. Hillis Miller, *The Disappearance of God: Five Nineteenth Century Writers* (Cambridge, Mass.: Harvard University Press, 1963).

II.

THE WORD
"GOD"

In our reflections we are dealing with the conjunction of a known factor and an unknown one. What we have to understand by "word" is considered self-evident. And today, in a way equally self-evident, it is held that what we must understand by the term "God" is problematic if not indeed unintelligible. When we now give special attention to the word "God," it is customary to distinguish between the word's known and unknown aspects, i.e., that the vocable as a mere linguistic form is certainly familiar to us, but that God as the content designated thereby is an entirely open question.

On such a presupposition as this, it is certainly pointless to expect that reflection on the nature of word will lead to an understanding of what "God" means. On the contrary, the conception of language here, naively presupposed as self-evident, necessarily makes the term "God" and therewith all talk of God meaningless. This understanding of language, however, also proves to be inadequate, quite apart from the question of God. It is a constriction which, consistently applied, strangles the life out of language.

The prevailing view of language is oriented towards the significatory function of words. The word is regarded as the sign—the spoken or written sign—with a concrete referent. This significatory view, based on the distinction between *signum* and *res,* comes from classical times. It determines the traditional form of grammatical and metaphysical thinking and has also become a standard factor

16

in the tradition of theological thought. The modern age has not eliminated this approach to the understanding of language; on the contrary it has sharpened it. Classical philosophy itself, but more especially the biblical tradition, had long prevented a one-sided development of this significatory concept of language. By this means it was modified—though to be sure also obscured—so that its dubiety was not consciously recognized. With the dawn of the modern age, the corrective function of these counter-forces was increasingly eliminated. Thus the path was clear for an unrestricted development of the mere sign-function of language. The logical result is that words are reduced to ciphers and functions, and syntax to a question of calculus.

The traditional view of language, and also the consistent mathematical treatment of it, doubtless contain elements of truth which cannot be abandoned. Their successful application in dictionaries and grammars, and now most recently in computers and in the science of cybernetics, is undeniable. This aspect of language, and the possibilities embraced in it, are not, however, the key to the essence of language. We are dealing here with an abstraction —to a certain extent a justified and necessary abstraction —from the humanity of language. To regard language exclusively as a technical instrument is to cut it off from that which is the constant source of its life—namely, the element of time.

Time, the very factor which is constitutive for the living event of language, is of secondary importance for the significatory understanding of language. However true it is that in formalized language temporal things can become the object of calculation, for the mathematical understanding of language as such, time is irrelevant. The constitutive significance of time for the reality of language can nevertheless be shown as follows. From the standpoint

17

of the use of language, the basic linguistic phenomenon is not the vocable as an isolated sign for an equally isolated thing. The individual vocable certainly does designate something, but when spoken it does not yet say anything. The basic unit of meaning in language is the sentence, which pieces together a subject in the medium of time. If a man utters not only a single vocable—unless of course it is an exclamation, and, even then, as such it implies a temporally determined sentence—but rather says a word, then he makes a statement of time. Word as spoken is always temporal word. Furthermore, the relation between the time stated and the time of the speaker himself is one of perspective. Yesterday I spoke of that which is happening today in the future tense, and tomorrow I shall speak of the same thing in the past tense. Thus not only what is stated is temporal, but also the statement itself. It is no accident that the genuine organ of language is the audible sound. The very fleetingness of the sound suits its purpose.

Word takes place as a temporal event. Thus to word there belongs the situation from which it arises, into which it comes, and which it changes. Accordingly, speaking also undergoes concrete modifications in a variety of ways —as address or promise, as instruction or conversation, as questioning or calling for help, as complaining or accusing, as cursing or praying.

The word situation parallels responsibility for the word.[1] The man who wishes to say something must have something to say and must allow himself to be taken at his word. Every word has its time. The man who says something must know whether it is the time for it. And in every case the word comes from the experience which has

[1] Cf. my essay, "Theology and the Evidentness of the Ethical," trans. James W. Leitch, *Translating Theology into the Modern Age* ("Journal for Theology and Church," 2), Robert W. Funk, ed., (New York: Harper & Row, 1965), pp. 96-129, esp. pp. 117 ff.

been given through time and which is based on the experience of time itself. Indeed we can speak only because language has been handed down to us and taught us and because only thus has experience of the world been opened up to us. The necessity and power of human language is ultimately determined by the fact that the world is experienced as time. I do not merely in a factual sense *have* a past and a future like all temporal things, but I also *know* of this. It is solely through language that I can have a relation to past and future, that past and future are present to me, that I can go back behind my present and stretch out ahead of it. Indeed, I not only *can* do this, I *must* do it. Because I am knowingly delivered over to time, I must take up my position towards past and future and answer for myself in my relation to time. It is not the concept of signification, but far more profoundly the concept of answerability that points us to that which is fundamental in language. Here we are provided with important points for the rest of our study.

When we speak of "word," we normally mean not the vocable—the atom of a specific linguistic system—but the totality of a statement. But by this is meant not the abstract linguistic constructions which grammar and logic are accustomed to use as model sentences. On the contrary, we have in mind word as an event, and thus word as inclusive of its relationship to its historical contexts, i.e., to the situation in which it is answered for. We must not by any means hastily reduce word to mere talk as distinct from action. According to the particular circumstances, conduct can be a decisive ingredient of the word, as a sort of sounding board for the word or a commentary on it. Conduct, moreover, can itself be acted word. In fact, a deed can be more eloquent than any word. And contrariwise, a mere word can be a deed. Let us therefore beware of a primitive antithesis between word and reality!

There must be constant awareness, however, of the difference between word as valid action, and word as escape or substitute for action.

19

We are really on the track of the phenomenon of word, however, only when we pass over superficial answers and insist on asking: What happens through the word? In view of the everyday use of language the answer might be, understanding in human relationships. On the other hand, in view of the use of language in the exact sciences one could say, information and the processing of information. Yet both answers compel us to ask further: What end is served by such use of language? In the second case a comprehensive answer appears to be simple, namely, that the collecting and processing of information should make it possible to calculate the future and hence to manipulate it. But what is that future over which we seek power? [2] This question brings us inevitably back to the first case

[2] The idea of cybernetics logically culminates in the technical manufacture (*Herstellung*) and programming of human nature, that is, in a "grasping at the future" which has complete control over the man who is oriented towards the future. But what would be accomplished if this were achieved? Cf. K. Steinbuch, *Automat und Mensch: Kybernetische Tatsachen und Hypothesen* (3rd ed.; Berlin and Heidelberg, Springer, 1965). The cybernetician still looks with a mixture of amazement and envy upon nature's advance over technology: "For an engineer it is simply astonishing what abilities nature could pack into the small space of the human skull. Measured by the number of gearing elements, the human brain is far superior to the greatest of contemporary computers" (Steinbuch, p. 23). But the goal is clear: "For our considerations it would be of incalculable value if a technical system comparable to the size and complexity of the human nervous system (etc.) could be manufactured. Would such a system then have psychic experiences, memory, emotions, etc.? Or, more precisely stated, would these questions credibly be answered with 'Yes'? The experiment is still several decades off; nonetheless we can expect that—*cum grano salis*—it will be made within the next two hundred years. It is, then, an *experimentum crucis* for or against the thesis of cybernetics" (Steinbuch, p. 10). Fantasy concerning the power of cybernetics to determine the future, and also concerning the goal of this power over the future, may be stimulated by an observation such as the following: "To me the difference between programming a machine (*Automaten*) for a highly skilled activity and training an apprentice is purely an external one" (Steinbuch, p. 4). See also R. Jungk and H. J. Mundt (eds.), *Der Griff nach der Zukunft: Planen und Freiheit* ("Modelle für eine neue Welt" [Munich and Basel: Kurt Desch, 1964]).

where the question is that of understanding among men. Why is understanding among men necessary? Here, too, we go straight to the heart of the matter: Men in their thinking and willing are incalculable and therefore become each other's adversaries. The attempt can of course also be made to make men calculable and tractable. But to the extent that such an attempt succeeds, it destroys the human thing about man—namely, his freedom. This corresponds exactly to the question of the future; i.e., to the extent that we succeed in getting the future securely in our grip, it loses its character as future.

And now, it is this that ultimately and properly speaking must happen, and can only happen, through our word: that future is granted, that freedom is granted. To be sure, in a provisional sense future and freedom can be granted by means of specific measures—as, for example, by rescuing a drowning man or liberating a prisoner. In this context the cybernetic use of language which intends to establish specific living conditions certainly also has an important function in the granting of future and freedom. Nevertheless, the establishment of specific living conditions is not by itself a guarantee of future and freedom. By saving a man from drowning, I do not save him from the despair of the future which drove him to attempt suicide. On the contrary, unless something else happens I merely maintain him in his futureless state. Likewise, I do not bestow freedom on a man who is thirsting for murder by letting him loose and so abandoning him to the force of his frenzy. Future and freedom are not things we possess like an object—such as money in our purse—or like an inborn or acquired capacity—such as the use of our senses and limbs. The time that still remains for me to live does not in itself mean I am granted a future, and the elbow-room that is open to me does not as such mean I am granted freedom. The crucial thing is the attitude I adopt

21

towards these things, the use I make of the time and space apportioned to me, whether I let the future be future and freedom be freedom, whether I truly acknowledge them to be what in truth they are.

Is this merely a matter of protection from the loss of future and the loss of freedom through external threats? Is it not rather a question of the fact that the very future and freedom which we possess are themselves the source of that which threatens our future and our freedom? Indeed, to put it still more plainly, is not what we usually call future merely the liquidation of our already lost future, and what we usually call freedom merely the liquidation of our already forfeited freedom? This does not cancel the fact that as long as he lives man does in fact have a future and has it so securely that death, that radical loss of future, is always felt to be a road into the dark and is thus itself understood under the category of the future. It is only on the ground of this indestructible relation of man to the future that the concept of a "lost future" has any meaning. Likewise, the concept of "lost freedom," rightly understood, does not exclude but includes the fact that freedom belongs to man as a thing that cannot be lost. Such loss is therefore something that cannot be forgotten; it continues to pain like an open wound. But when the loss of future and freedom is no longer a mere possibility but already an accomplished fact, then and only then does what can give future and freedom to the man who has lost future and freedom become a really burning question.

Only word can do this. That is already indicated by our compulsion to inquire about the truth of future and freedom and about their true realization. Truth is the realm of language. It is only because man has the gift of language that the question of truth arises for him. And at the same time, to be sure, the question of falsehood also arises. A beast, or certainly a stone, cannot lie, because for it the question of truth does not arise. It is only because man can speak that there is any question of whether he tells the truth or whether he lies. The most elementary answer to the question of the purpose served by word is that it serves to tell the truth. Falsehood is misuse of language, corrupt and corrupting word. Truth is sound and healing word.

But what does it mean to tell the truth? In the first instance it manifestly means to set reality into words. This process could be compared, say, with the fact that a precious stone shows to full advantage only when it is properly cut and set. Truth is reality set in words, and thus the making known of that which—as command and promise—is the mystery of reality. This does not cause the mystery to disappear, rather it causes it to emerge precisely as a mystery, i.e., as something which gives men food for thought and for faith, for hope and for love. These are the basic human forms of conduct, the forms of reverence for the mystery of reality. To be sure, human existence also involves, seemingly first and foremost, the effort, either crude or subtle, to lay hold of unveiled, immediate reality, to plan and dominate, possess and enjoy, press on and break records. But this effort to lay hold of naked immediacy misses reality unless it is bridled through our being grasped by that which can only be a matter of hearing and waiting, and is thus a matter of word.

Telling the truth is therefore something more than the stating of correct facts. This is, of course, also important; but it does not provide the standard, so that everything else would, according to individual taste, be a fine but not determinative superstructure. The correct stating of limited facts which settles individual questions is related to telling the truth, which as such gives us an openness towards the mystery, as a special activity is related to life.

23

The task of word therefore consists in attacking the root of its own misuse and making man himself true.

The criterion of the truth which makes man himself true is that it makes him free. For freedom, too, is dependent upon language. As the rational animal who has the gift of language, man is given the freedom of being able to decide, is released from the compulsion of his instincts and the pressure of the immediate present, and is given space in which to choose—not indeed to choose as he pleases, however. He *must* make use of his freedom, even if only to throw it away and thereby lose himself. And he *must* take responsibility for his freedom, even if only by means of irresponsible evasions. Lies are the perverse attempt to gain back by means of word the lost elbowroom of one's freedom. This merely underlines the fact that freedom is dependent on word—and all the more so when it is a case of helping the man who has lost his freedom back to freedom. It is true that the use of force can to a certain extent destroy freedom, but it cannot create freedom. Freedom can only be *called* into being as one literally "speaks freedom" to his neighbor, i.e., speaks to him in such a way that freedom is passed to him and he is enabled to enter into the field of freedom.

To be sure, the question is now thrust compellingly upon us: What sort of word has this kind of liberating power, this authority to make man true? But let us be patient and continue to persevere with our prior question: What is it that happens through the word? What is it that makes word, and word alone, suited to make man true and to make him free?

Let us give an even sharper edge to the insights already gained by now observing that it is the business of word to make present what is not at hand, what is absent. To be sure, this is in a way also accomplished by a picture, a symbol, a memento, or a relic. But in all these instances there is the danger of an illusion, namely, of the mediated presence being confused with immediate presence. Moreover, in such cases the absence of the thing represented is only of an accidental and temporal kind, and it is only the added interpretation through the word that can make clear what is really meant. For it is the business of words alone to make present what is even utterly hidden.

Everything that is expressed in language is dependent on language only to the extent that hiddenness is involved in one respect or another. However true it may be that our language cannot say everything, because many things are beyond its reach and call for silence, there is nevertheless all the more need to underline the experience, banal and trite as it has become, that language can say infinitely more than is perceived by the senses. From this point of view the convenient distinction between nature and history (in the strict sense of human history) is made more sharp in that reality is deeply hidden in space and time and is therefore abundantly rich in language and strains ever anew towards language.

The primary experience of the hiddenness of historic reality is the remembrance of decisions that have been made and the awaiting of decisions as yet unknown. The former is the field of thankfulness and remorse, the latter that of anxiety and hope. Although the hiddenness of the future is more oppressing, and the desire for a word that grants a future more burning than the need to lighten the darkness of the past and to become free from it, we ultimately have here a single interwoven mystery that embraces past and future and knocks at the door of the present. The word that makes us true and makes us free and therefore grants us a future will in no case lead us on a flight into illusion; but from the truth of what has happened in the past, it will invest us with an assurance

25

for that future which is superior to all dwindling and disappointing futures.

Where have our reflections on language and word brought us? I answer: into the realm of the experience of what we mean when we say "God." That sounds like a daring remark and requires some explanation.

The purpose of our undertaking was not to set up a general theory of language in order then to apply it as a special case to our talk of God. Rather, our concern has been to characterize the situation in which man finds himself in virtue of the fact that he has the gift of language. That is to say, since man is rightly called the being who has the gift of language, we have been concerned to take the nature of language as the ground on which to define his basic situation. This has brought us into the situation which is addressed as and intended by the word "God."

The shocking thing about this is, first of all, the suspicion that here the fatal attempt is being made to renew the absurd enterprise of proving God. To have shown the absurdity of that enterprise is generally held to be the one thing which despite all hostilities still unites the theology and philosophy of modern times. Our project does in fact bear a formal resemblance to the way in which Thomas Aquinas answers the question of the existence of God.[3] He radicalizes our experience of the world in various ways, until he finally claims to have reached that which is generally addressed as "God." Whatever the critic may have to say of this, it is hardly possible to understand even Thomas' undertaking as being in the usual sense a proof of the existence of God. But it does seek to show what the word "God" means. This attempt would have

[3] Cf. my essays, "Der hermeneutische Ort der Gotteslehre bei Petrus Lombardus und Thomas von Aquin," *Zeitschrift für Theologie und Kirche,* 61 (1964), pp. 283-326, and "Existenz zwischen Gott und Gott. Ein Beitrag zur Frage nach der Existenz Gottes," *Ibid.,* 62 (1965), pp. 86-113, especially pp. 95-100.

to be submitted to a searching interpretation if it is to be rightly understood. It may be criticized as misleading. Yet whoever takes the word "God" upon his lips cannot possibly refuse to give an account of what he means by it. And moreover, it must be an account which points to an area of universal human experience. The present-day crisis in regard to the word "God"—if indeed it is a crisis at all and not an already concluded death-agony—can be surmounted only when the meaning of the word "God" is verifiable.

But that which is suggested by the claim to verify the word "God" may be even more shocking. The meaning of the word "God," we might venture to say in review, is the basic situation of man as word situation.[4] By normal

[4] This statement necessarily becomes false when it is construed as a definition. For the traditional metaphysical doctrine of God it was axiomatic that God is indefinable: "It is clear . . . that God has neither genus nor differences, and that there is no definition of God, nor any way of demonstrating him through his effects. For definition is by means of genus and difference, and definition is the means of demonstration." Thomas Aquinas, *Summa Theologica* I, Q. 3, Art. 5. *Nature and Grace—Selections from the Summa Theologica of Thomas Aquinas,* ed. and trans. A. M. Fairweather ("The Library of Christian Classics," Vol. XI [Philadelphia: Westminster, 1954]), p. 65. Today the logician would base the indefinability of God on the ground that "God" is not an *Autosemantikon* but a *Synsemantikon,* a word which receives meaning through the way it is used. (For this allusion I am indebted to Professor Paul Lorenzen of Erlangen with whom I met in Austin, Texas in connection with these lectures.) My attempts to formulate the above sentence through the non-use of the copula led, unfortunately, to the weakening of its scope. I request that the sentence be read as a direction (*als eine Wegweisung*) for the use of the word "God." Cf. above, pp. 10-11 and Ludwig Wittgenstein's famous statement that "the meaning of a word is its use in the language" ("Die Bedeutung eines Wortes ist sein Gebrauch in der Sprache"). *Philosophical Investigations I,* trans. G. E. M. Anscombe (Oxford: Basil Blackwell, 1958), No. 43, p. 20e. As far as the rest is concerned, let one free himself from the prejudice of an actualistic understanding of "situation" as well as from an isolationistic speaking of man. On the basis of the biblical witness concerning God as creator and redeemer, or of dogmatic speaking of God as *principium* and *finis* (Cf. Thomas Aquinas, *Summa Theologica* I, Q. 1, Art. 7), or of Luther's use of the

27

standards it is offensive to assert that God is a situation, and not only that but the basic situation of man. There arise at once the familiar objections that ontological statements are here actually dissolved and theology reduced to anthropology. Whoever measures and sharpens his responsibility for talk of God on the unaltered present, however, will not easily be content with or give in to schemes of this sort.

Our suggestion concerning the proper understanding of the word "God" calls us, in the first instance, to consider the fact that there is no question at all here of understanding "God" in the usual sense of a content distinct from the word itself—a sort of speechless thing that has to be brought into the language by being named, that is, designated by a vocable. On the contrary, it is here a question of God himself as Word. That is to say, the vocable "God" points to a word event that is always already in full swing. Pious mistrust of such statements could be countered by observing that according to the Trinitarian faith the Word is the Second Person of the Godhead, that God himself is thus intrinsically word and not something which, in itself wordless, must first be placed by external means in the field of language in order to become an object of word. Yet this role of the word in the doctrine of the Trinity, though highly important, must not now make us flee from the open field in which we have been moving in order to seek refuge behind the sheltering walls of ecclesiastical dogma.

If the word "God" means the basic situation of man as word situation, then by speaking of God one perceives man at the point of his linguisticality. And indeed the

formula *coram Deo* (Cf. my *Luther: Einführung in sein Denken* [Tübingen: Mohr, 1964] especially pp. 227 ff.), the intention of the above statement is confirmed. The application of the situational concept corresponds to the sense of the formula, "between God and God" (see above, p. 26, note 3).

word "God" shows us that man in his linguisticality is not master of himself. He lives from the power of a word that is not his own, and at the same time he thirsts after the power of a word that likewise cannot be his own.

This fact, that man precisely in his linguisticality is not essentially self-sufficient, is illustrated by his dependence on his fellow man. No one can speak independently. And no one can be content to speak alone. Man speaks because he has received the gift of language as taught to him by others, and because he longs to hear in turn an echo, an answer to his own speaking.

This fact, that man as the being who has the gift of language is entwined in an immeasurably vast network of human events, has countless aspects which we cannot here define or even indicate. But it is obvious that the total word event, in which the participation of the individual is like a drop in the bucket, cannot be adequately interpreted from the standpoint of co-humanity. To be sure, the dimension of the individual cannot be excluded from anything that has to do with language, either from the mysterious transformations of language on the large scale or from the hidden conversation of the heart with itself. Yet precisely these two perspectives, the macroscopic and the microscopic aspects of the word event, bring to our attention the fact that in every word event there is present a depth dimension which is indicated by the word "God" —not, so to speak, as a prolongation of the causal series into the adjacent realm of the hyper-macrocosmic and the hyper-microcosmic, but as a hidden and tacit word event to which every word owes its existence.

That it is precisely in that which is the sign of his power —namely, his language—that man reveals himself not to be his own master, is a lesson which we can never learn thoroughly enough. It is a lesson which may be primarily taught to us by answering these two questions: What empowers us to use word? And, what is the power of word?

The question of what empowers us to use word forces us to realize that man participates in word in the form of answerability. That is to say, he has neither the first word nor the last. He is summoned to word, so that his word is always only an answer. And he in turn has to answer for this answer: he has to await a judgment to which he can add nothing. But summons and judgment derive their power from bestowal and acceptance. How little man in his linguisticality is his own master is experienced most impressively in his dependence on the gift of word, on the permission, the freedom to speak a good, right, helpful, salutary word. It is wholly legitimate to illustrate this by the fact that responsible speaking comes from the silence of listening, and that finding the right word has the character of a sudden bright idea or a happy inspiration. And it may be illustrated further by the fact that man cannot by his word compel understanding, but must wait to see if and when the scattered seed springs up.

The second question, concerning the power of word, recalls once more what we have already said—namely, that it is the business of word to make present what is not at hand. The fact that word brings to us what is past and future, and us to it, is only an illustration of the way in which man is dependent on confrontation by a word that comes his way, that liberates him both from the frightening restrictions that bind him to what is present and from the anxiety of his own heart, and that thus frees him for the things which are outside his power to command but are offered to him to believe. Man needs language more for hearing than for speaking, for believing than for acting. For this reason the extreme situation which man is absolutely unable even slightly to change—namely, bondage to sin and death—puts word to the test: whether man is abandoned to that which renders him speechless, or whether even in muteness he can still cling to a word that sets him outside himself.

The word situation as the basic situation of man makes it plain that because he lives by the word man is ultimately not a doer but a receiver. Although he is able to objectify all things from a neutral distance, he himself cannot escape into neutrality. However much he is and in all respects remains at the mercy of the world and his fellowmen, yet in all these relations he is nevertheless himself, a responsible individual, a person come of age, called to assert and maintain by a right use of the word that mystery of reality which surrounds him and constitutes his true situation. If we said before that the word "God" means the basic situation of man as word situation, then we can now also say: "God" is the mystery of reality.

Yet what right have we to call this "God"? It is true, in any event, that what we finally said about the basic situation of man certainly harmonizes with the fact that the word "God" addresses man and demands that he be a receiver, tolerates no neutrality, and expects from man a responsible account of all that concerns him. But do not the traditional representations of God prevent us from using this word—a word which can be rightly used only with a good conscience, and which insincerity misuses? I do not refer merely to pagan or childish representations of God as an animal or as bearded, or to the Trinitarian picture of two men with a dove, but also to the metaphysical concept of God as *ens realissimum* and *causa sui,* and indeed even to Jesus' talk of God the Father, and to the church's talk of the Father of Jesus Christ.

Representations of God, to be sure, give expression to that which is meant by the word "God" only to the extent that they *present man to God,* and thus awaken man to his basic situation. The moment the word situation of which

31

we have spoken is abandoned and God is regarded in one way or another as reality, rather than as the mystery of reality which lays exacting hold upon us, then God is murdered.

Yet what can the vocable "God" do to prevent this? Is it not in any case so ambiguous and so unclear that it no longer means anything to the man who is seeking clear concepts and precise definitions? The classical Christian doctrine of God, it is true, has always declared the indefinability of God to be in accordance with the nature of God. But it has also always seen in this the reason why the word "God" gives endless food for thought. The apparent lack of sharply defined meaning is a thing this word shares with all terms which are not labels for finished products, but are rather summonses which require of man an inner movement for which the word in question only points the direction. The movement thus required of man by the word "God" is known in that situation in which the genuine use of "God" is that of the vocative, of address.

To be sure, the warrant to use the word "God" in order to call upon God cannot be derived from the vocable "God." For this, it is necessary that God becomes audible in the word. The meaning of the word "God" is not to be believed apart from the word of God.

III.

THE WORD
OF GOD

The meaning of the word "God" is determined by its use, or to be more precise, by the necessity of using the word "God." To use a vocable means to make use of it along with other words to form a coherent statement. A necessary use of the word "God" is accordingly one which takes place in a connected statement, in a word event, for the clarity of which it is required that God be named as that to which the word event in question relates, to which it refers, to which it appeals, from which it derives its truth. The vocable "God"—so far as it has any meaning at all —belongs to a verbal whole which necessarily belongs to God. In short, the word "God" requires the word of God, as the word of God requires the word "God."

The way we have indulged almost in a verbal play on the two expressions "the word 'God' " and "the word of God," together with the pregnant brevity in which we have stated the fact of their belonging together, can easily delude us into overlooking the long and arduous path from the one to the other. An account of this constitutes the last stage of our reflections on God and word.

In the context of the language of our day, "word of God" seems to be traditional language, and it is problematic whether and how far it can still be the language of today. The sense of alienation affects not merely the vocable "God," nor the concept "word of God"; it affects the whole complex of what, with the claim to be word of God, has been handed down in the form of scripture and continues to be handed on in the form of preaching. To

33

a certain extent there is indeed a rising curve of alienation —from the use of the vocable "God" to the claim of a man to speak in the name of God. Yet we must ask what is the source of this alienation from what was once an obvious matter of course. Has preaching lost its authority because the word "God" has become unintelligible, or has the word "God" become an empty term because preaching turned empty? The impression that we are using a foreign language when it comes to the word of God certainly does not arise from the fact that God is taken seriously as the one who is "wholly other" and therefore foreign to man. On the contrary, the alienating element is interpreted without more ado as the sign of a false claim. Accordingly, as the case may be, we emphasize that we have here an antiquated, or inexact, pre-scientific language, or a group language—namely, a church language which is of importance only for the initiated.

In this assessment of the situation right and wrong elements are confusingly entangled. It is certainly right that we have our talk of God from the tradition. Had we never heard any talk of God—an absurd hypothesis!—we could hardly conceive it on our own. It is therefore understandable that the impression arises that our concern with the word "God" and the word of God is nothing but an expression of the fact that we have not yet overcome the hampering bonds of tradition, and that this concern results in an allegorical dislocation—the painful attempt to combine two fundamentally different languages and artificially to harmonize their contradictions.

It is, moreover, unfortunately true that Christian proclamation has largely become a ghetto language. Seen superficially, to be sure, it has not by any means been driven out of public life; but in actual fact it has assumed the character of a group language for private use. The language of public life on the other hand, the language of

34

the workaday world of politics, economics and industry, of science and culture, has been secularized and has become on the whole so technical that the word of God is entirely out of place in it. Apart from noncommittal forms of speech, talk of God is confined to specially reserved, institutional places and occasions—Sunday worship, religious education, marriages and funerals, religious papers or the religious column in the daily press, particular hours on radio and television, and so on. Amid the plurality of languages in modern society, talk of God occupies only one narrow sector, and is itself in turn split into many dialects. In consequence of this multiplicity such talk is made into a technical instrument for the cultivation of particular special traditions, and thus scarcely can it any longer profess unreservedly to be the word of God—unless this claim, too, has shrunk to the status of a traditional label. Outside of the appointed reserves it is extraordinarily difficult even in intimate circles to use the word "God" at all. Even there talk of God has often degenerated into a scanty element of custom, say, in the form of grace before meals, or as a part of the conventional style for congratulation or condolence. As for how much the word "God" is used in prayer and the word of God read and meditated upon in the privacy of individual life, here there are—I hope!—no statistics to divulge the facts.

The problems arising out of this situation cannot really be solved by modernizing our vocabulary, or by calling for a courageous confession of the faith. Both are in a limited sense right enough. But they are only treatments of the external symptoms. To expect too much from them is only to cause trouble. Coloring our language with splashes of alluring jargon underlines a lack of confidence in the word, which is fatal to Christian proclamation. And the word of God—prohibiting as it does all self-assertion

35

by man in the face of God—can only be falsified by the activities of the propagandist.

The difficulties which are involved today in the use of the word "God" and in the proclamation of the word of God are not external, but belong intrinsically to the subject itself. And this indeed is most closely bound to the question of the appropriate situation. Much more than we generally admit, our life is strongly determined by the conditions of the age of technology and the masses. Consequently, the basic situation of man, which we have characterized as word situation, is on the one hand very largely pushed into the background; on the other hand and for that very reason it stands out all the more sharply when we are forced to notice it. The technical approach to reality depends on the toning down both of the mystery of reality and of man's involvement in it. Because the basic situation of man is abandoned to silence, which in turn creates further silence, the increasing technical use of our language brings its increasing impoverishment. Similarly, mass society causes the stunting of individual responsibility. The expressing of life in routine patterns can of course lead to a greater isolating or atomizing of existence. Man is then left helpless and speechless.

The word which is to bring help into this situation, however, must submit to the most stringent test of its guarantee of certainty. In the days when Christian faith was publicly recognized as a matter of course, existing principles of thought and established conditions of authority vouched for the legitimacy of the claim of the word of God. Now, however, our talk of God must secure for itself the recognition which it claims. Authority is now a question of the authorship of evidence and respect. And our assent to and agreement with such a demanding word depends on whether the basic situation described above is convincingly expressed in contrast to the situation of the technical approach to the world.

The examination of these relationships enjoins us to prudence. The rationalization and technification of public and largely also of private life, has created an abundance of situations which have been sterilized, so to speak, against a germinating of the basic situation of man, and have thus been made unfruitful for talk of God. This process we have to recognize as a fact, and we must even allow it a certain legitimacy. The reality of human life is not such that the basic situation of man is or could be constantly exposed. At least part of the reason for the disappearance of talk of God lies in a not unjustified sense of shame which is sensitive towards the trivializing of what is extraordinary and tremendous. Hence it is a healthy modesty that compels us to acquire a faculty of discrimination and to learn when it is the right time—and that means, when it is necessary—to speak of God.

At the same time, the reserving of separate occasions for the word of God, or even the forcing of it into the private sphere, are not by any means only to be discredited as reprehensible signs of decay. In light of the results of the comprehensive change in the public situation, we should recognize gratefully and modestly that amid the manifold phenomena of modern life these results do in any event grant us the existence of a form of Christian tradition. A sober evaluation of this kind could free us from much that is constricting in our efforts at proclamation as well as in the form of the church and of the Christian life. Christianity in its historical existence participates also in worldliness, precisely because Christian word, Christian community, and Christian existence are not by any means, if I may say so, word of God in fixed form. Simply and naturally, they are on standby duty in readiness not for any and every eventuality, but, whenever validly required, for the service of the word of God. For that very reason, to be sure, this involves the readiness to assume responsibility before the public and for the public, namely, the readiness to say plainly why it is necessary to use the word "God" and what the word is which authorizes us to do so.

Of course, this can happen only when we discard an idea which falsifies the whole picture—that is, the notion that a particular interest has to be supported in public life, that the cause and the continuance of a particular party has to be propagandized, that a uniformity of language has to be sought. Whoever, therefore, has grasped what is meant by "word of God" cannot be ridden by any sort of anxious concern for the word of God and ultimately therewith for God himself; he can only be driven to concern for man and for the world. It is so easy, of course, to believe that humanity maintains itself indestructibly in history, whereas the word of God is a rare and sensitive plant which belongs to tradition and must be preserved from extinction. The questions concerning the relationship of God and word accordingly appear to constitute a linguistic problem of a special kind, which concerns only those interested in the word of God. Indeed the phrase "word of God" itself appears to be such a linguistic problem. In contrast to this idea, which does in fact readily suggest itself, the very criterion of a right understanding lies in whether God's word is understood as assurance-giving language which has a saving effect in history, as the constant granting of the gift of language, as an authority for the word which is superior to the powers that render us speechless.

We look in the first instance simply to the historic fact of what comes to us from the biblical tradition. To be sure, there is here to a very great extent a conservative element at work—the reverent preserving and maintaining of a language whose original utterances are now two to three thousand years behind us. But this fact of astonishing linguistic continuity cannot be explained by conservatism—that disposition to let the past relieve one of one's own responsibility.

To be sure, the original word event which has taken fixed form in Holy Scripture appears to be a finished production which itself has become the object of further tradition. Yet it is in itself already a traditional event containing an extraordinary variety of movement. The twofold Christian canon of the Old and New Testaments confronts us with the acutely challenging question of its unity and its difference. It is precisely this transition from the Old to the New, with all its inexhaustible implications for thought, that constitutes its canonicity. But even the two parts taken separately do not represent handy units of tradition which would allow simple verbal repetition. Both Testaments embrace an abundance of historic statements. They cannot simply be added together to form a single system, but they are certainly related to each other as elements in a coherent tradition-event. The Old and New Testaments manifest a peculiar conformity with each other in that both are processes of the successive conferral of authority to proclaim the word to new situations, processes which ever grant and renew the gift of language. Neither is in itself simply that which is to be transmitted. On the contrary, the real object to be transmitted is that which remains the source of the word event, not allowing enclosure in merely one, exclusive, invariable linguistic form. The source of authorization can in both cases ultimately be indicated only by a name—in the Old Testament, Yahweh, in the New Testament, Jesus. And they have something else in common, that is, that both processes of tradition—to express it in a precise way, the traditions of the prophets and of the apostles—point beyond their own day to a continuing responsibility for proclamation which the word that has gone before us does not take off our shoulders, but rather opens to us. There is one difference however. It is only through the New Testament that the Old Testament is also incorporated into a universal traditional event, which enters into all languages in order to prepare them for the saving word event, that which is necessary for redemption.

Word of God, according to the biblical tradition, thus seeks to be understood as a word event that does not go out of date but constantly renews itself, does not create closed areas of special interest but opens up the world, does not enforce uniformity but is linguistically creative. Of course it is startling—but only because it reveals what was hidden. Certainly it is tradition, yet tradition of a kind that sets us free for our own present. Whatever is put forth as word of God is certainly changed into an antiquated, constricting word that enslaves us, and thus becomes the opposite of what the word of God is, whenever it is denied responsible participation in the word event.

Naturally, a thing is not word of God simply because it claims to be so. Yet it would be misleading to say that God's word requires verification—if by that we are thinking of an additional, externally given confirmation and evidence of its truth, as, for example, is given a witness's statement by an inspection of the scene of the crime, or a promise by its actual fulfillment in due course. On the contrary, God's word is itself verification. It verifies itself by verifying man.

In order to grasp the meaning of this, we must proceed from a simple point of hermeneutics: word is a means of understanding. That is to say, the linguistic utterance normally mediates understanding itself and does not first have to be made understandable. It is only when the normal function of word is disturbed that interpretation is required. The aim of such interpretation cannot, however, be anything other than the removal of the obstacle which prevents the word from mediating understanding by itself.

But now, here it is that the matter of *how* word mediates understanding is first brought properly to our attention. Briefly put, one could say that word brings about understanding by announcing in a familiar context something that is hidden. Two points are important. First, word always presupposes word, understanding always understanding. If instead of this we were to say, as would be perfectly correct, that word appeals to experience, then the experiential character of understanding and the linguistic character of experience is only emphasized. Hence, the field of experience into which a word is spoken can appropriately be designated as its context. That is one important point. The second is, word adds to what is familiar the announcement of what is hidden. Whatever the concrete way in which this relationship may present itself, understanding through word in any event involves something hidden coming to linguistic expression. Thus word also always presupposes something that has not been said, and understanding always presupposes something that has not been understood, in order, of course, to say it and understand it to the extent that this is possible. Yet this happens in such a way that what is merely announced in the word is understood as altering the context through the presence of what is hidden. If this is a matter of a change which is not to violate the context but rather to rectify and verify it, then that which is hidden, that which is spoken into the context and added to it, must correspond to that which is already hidden in the context and which is now identified as such and thereby brought to light. Thus there are two elements of hiddenness that correspond to each other—one arising in the context itself and one which is added to the context. That is also why the more fruitful form for disclosing the word's power to awaken understanding is not to spew forth platitudes but rather to allude to something that provokes reflection.

Furthermore, the Bible's word and the proclamation arising from it are obviously addressed to an appropriate context. Only in this way can what is said come to understanding. Thus the word which claims to be God's word always presupposes a corresponding word. And the understanding awakened by the word of God always refers to a corresponding understanding. At the same time, of course, there is also presupposed a lack of word and understanding—and because this happens "at the same time," it must give to the word and understanding already existing in the context the character of an antithetical correspondence, or a contradiction, provided that it is not a matter of supplementary word but of decisive word in the strict sense. God's word is in essence not that which merely supplements the context into which it enters. On the contrary, it renders a decision concerning it. And accordingly the hidden factor which is announced into the context by the word of God does not concern some aspect or other of the context, but rather the whole context itself. It renders a life and death decision.

Here theology seems to find itself in a dilemma. It may emphasize that the word of God always finds a previously given analogue, a "natural" knowledge of God, as it is then called, with which the revealed knowledge of God connects, a presupposed understanding to which the word of God relates. The simplest, and at the same time most effective argument for this consists in asking how God's word is to be proclaimed where the word "God" is not understood at all. Yet the inevitable consequence of this point of view appears to be that it diminishes the wonder of God's word, its indisposability, its power to make all things new, its character of grace. It becomes a word which only supplements its context and therefore, strictly speaking, does not deserve to be called word of God at all.

Or theology may emphasize the opposite pole. All forms of natural knowledge of God are bluntly rejected, and the use of the word "God" is held to be possible solely by virtue of the word of God. Any other procedure is condemned as a transformation of theology into anthropology, as a vain attempt to penetrate into the orbit of the word of God from without. Only when theology is securely established, so it is said, can we also address ourselves—and on that basis—to the theme of anthropology. The consequence of this view, however, is to render problematic the relation of the word of God to experience, to the reality that concerns man as man, to the world, and to history. We are threatened with a positivistic view of revelation which makes the word of God more of a supplement—and an unmotivated one at that—than ever. Or else we are faced with a *salto mortale* and, as a consistent way of eliminating natural theology in favor of Christology, we are urged to renounce the word "God" altogether.[1]

Good theology does not submit to the schematism of these positions, schematisms which suffer from false antitheses and the choice of mistaken battlegrounds. They have also, in point of fact, always been championed only to the accompaniment of auspicious inconsistencies—which, to be sure, have demanded the price paid in the unhappy course of the discussion.[2] The theologian's passion is more easily devoted to talking than to hearing, and expends itself in the impatience in which we talk past each

---

[1] Cf. Paul van Buren, *The Secular Meaning of the Gospel* (New York: Macmillan, 1963), especially pp. 81 ff.

[2] I am of the opinion that the disagreements which caused the break up of the circle around *Zwischen den Zeiten* ought to be critically re-examined.

other rather than in the patience with which we must listen to each other.

What is transmitted as word of God can thus be understood as word of God only when it finds in man and his world the context into which it announces something hidden; nor can this be just anything that happens to be hidden, but must be that which, hidden and announced as such—in short, as the truth—renders a decision concerning the humanity of man. The tradition of the word of God is thus not added to our experience in an unrelated juxtaposition or as a supplement to it, as something that supplants or embellishes our reality. Rather, the tradition of the word of God seeks to verify us where our being in the world is concerned—that is, according to the basic meaning of this Latin compound from *verum* and *facere* it seeks to "make true," to bring to the truth our being in the world. This is no mere wordplay; it rather takes seriously what is meant by *identification* in relation to the humanity of man. Where man is concerned, identification is verification.

The word of God verifies itself as *God's* word precisely by addressing man with a recognition of his basic situation as word situation, that is, with a recognition of the fact that man as man is always one who is already being approached by God. However man may interpret his encounter with the mystery of reality, the word of God charges him with the concealment, in one way or another, of his basic situation; it declares that he is not identical with himself, thus not in the truth, and that he is therefore lacking the freedom to be in harmony and peace with the mystery which has power over him. Otherwise, he would conform to that mystery with undivided heart, in faith, love, and hope, and so answer for all things by praising God. But man does not exist as the word that conforms to his basic situation—namely, as affirmative answer to

44

God. Because he is not at one with God, he is not at one with himself. As one who is godless, he is man existing in contradiction.

The basic situation of man cannot be regarded in abstraction, in separation from the concretions beneath which it is concealed, ignored, or forgotten. On the contrary, the word of God brings this basic situation to expression precisely in its concretions. That is why the language of the Bible is so rich and so close to reality. This is felt even by those who do not perceive the word of God in the Bible. Above all, however, that this is the Bible's way of speaking results in the fact that the announcement of what is hidden takes place not as theoretic enlightenment or as an appeal for the realization of an ideal, but in such a way that man is transposed into his basic situation as word situation. The Bible's way of saying this is to place man before God; that is to say, the word of God alters the situation decisively. It does so by placing man in a concrete word situation which makes him open to his basic situation; it does so through a word of faith that testifies to love and therefore awakens hope. This is why the word of God is uttered historically and is inseparable from narrative, appearing in its fullness as man, as the man Jesus. To believe in him means to be transposed in him into our own basic situation. This is no artificial substitute, but a promising fulfillment. For the truth that makes man true lies outside himself—that is his basic situation.

Why is it that this word which makes man true, and is therefore a saving word necessary for redemption, must be called "word of God"? To what extent is the word "God" essential to the clarity of this word event? Is it not, on the contrary, a hindrance to it? Are we not compelled first of all laboriously to make clear what really ought to serve the purposes of clarity but manifestly does not do so, or at all events no longer does so? It appears in fact as though the word "God" was able to advance the clarity of the saving word as long as it belonged to the things generally accepted as a matter of course. It does indeed have such an overwhelmingly strong hold on the language of the Bible and of church tradition that many find the very question before us to be itself sacrilegious. Yet no one can deny the fact that the word "God" is not simply a biblical or even a Christian word. It refracts all kinds of religious colors. Claims made for the word to which the Bible testifies as word of God involve a never ending battle for the word "God." The word of God understood in that way is the constant de-idolization of the word "God." Precisely this process caused the word "God" to advance the clarity of the word of God. The historical context of the biblical message was, of course, from the very outset the factual misuse of the name of God.

But must we not draw the consistent conclusion from the changed situation in regard to the word "God"? Does the use of it not restrict Christian proclamation to the circle of those who are still familiar with the word "God" today? Does not that proclamation automatically shut itself off from the vast number to whom the word "God" has become so foreign that faith seems to them a demand for submission to the law of a bygone age? We must take very seriously the question of whether the word "God" does not today bar the way of the word of God to the world. We must even go on to ask still more critically: Does the traditional use of the word "God" not carry with it from its sources in general religion a force of its own, against which the word to which the Bible testifies as gospel has been able only exceptionally, but not permanently, to assert itself purely and savingly? Did not the Christian tradition in some ways grow up in danger because of its use of the word "God"?

Fully aware of such dangers, as they have always existed, we address ourselves once more to the problem which especially concerns our age. We must at all times beware of shortsighted distortions. What causes the traditional understanding of the word "God" to appear obsolete today is partly the result of defective interpretation. If the vocable "God" with its customary associations is set immediately in the context of modern thought, without regard to the thought forms of an earlier age, then the result is a caricature which must not be described as the genuine view of the tradition. Yet even when allowance is made for the change of context, there still remains the difference that formerly the word of God had to rescue the word "God" from idolization, whereas today the word of God has to rescue God himself from anonymity and pseudonymity. If what we have said concerning the basic situation of man as word situation and concerning the indication this provides for the meaning of the word "God" is true, then our task is to take what has subsided into speechlessness, or has been suppressed in superficial talk, and help it anew to linguistic expression. It would be senseless to renounce the use of the vocable "God" for this task. Not for its own sake should it be used, but in order to save man from choking on his own self because he no longer has any word with which to cry out of the depths of his self-contradiction and call upon the mystery that surrounds him. The vocable "God" is therefore by no means to be replaced by another, but it does have to be intensively interpreted within the field of experience and thereby be brought back again to the situation in which its use is essential.

This, to be sure, is not a matter of forming and executing a well-aimed plan of action. What we can do to effect this has at best the character of a standby service which is ready for an event that is not in our power. The enormity of the task dawns upon us when we consider the fullness of tradition in which we have to immerse ourselves, when we also hold ourselves open to the tempestuous vehemence of our age, which is the place of present responsibility, and when we bring both together in the truthfulness which respect for the profound mystery of reality demands of us. The standby service of which we have spoken consists in concentration upon the biblical word of God, not by withdrawal into a comfortable linguistic shell, but by stepping out into the world in confident reliance upon a new authority to speak. When it comes to the inevitable reduction to things that are few but genuine, this authority does not spare us shock and pain—but it is also not without the liberating experience of certainty.

Preparing to regain the word "God" from the word of God is at all meaningful and necessary only because we are concerned with the world. As ecclesiastical traditionalists or religious individualists we could content ourselves with the customary understanding of the word "God"—or indeed we could also manage without this vocable. Responsibility before the public and for the public, however, makes it a duty clearly to identify by name—and by a single name at that—the truth of that power which drives man and holds him in the restlessness of his self-contradiction, and the truth which promises eternal peace.

The word of Holy Scripture discloses that which on a thousand occasions man may experience as his situation:

This is, first, a divided reality which in its dichotomy does, to be sure, assume the most varied configurations, but which possesses its unity and its gravity in the fact that it is the *one* reality, whose signature is the tension of the enigmatic and the mysterious.

Secondly, it is a reality of a verbal kind which surges in all directions in inexhaustible multiplicity, but is directed as it were towards man, laying hold of him at the point of his verbal responsibility and causing him—amid the fullness of what is unspeakable, or in the straits of what makes him speechless—to cry out to Him whom he entreats and from whom he receives—even in the midst of the annihilating challenge of that which is incomprehensible—the grace of a word that grants life.

Thirdly, it is a reality which demands faith—a faith about which there are confused interpretations that lead men astray and falsify its concealed truth—the bringing of which to truth and reality is promised to the word which receives its authority from Jesus.

To be able to call this situation of man by a name—to be able to use a single word to indicate both its enigmatic obscurity and the light that shines in it and is not swallowed up by the darkness—is necessary for life itself. For only so is the saving word to be proclaimed as word of God, and that means, as word for the godless. And only so is language in general to preserve its humanity. But then even in the word of the godless there is to be heard a hidden word of God.

INDEX

Type, 10 on 12 Times Roman
Display, Tempo
Paper, White "R" Antique